T0087625

# Great American Songwriters
## Seven Piano Duets
### Arrangements by
### Jim Lyke

Edited by
**Robert Pace**

*Many Thanks to Lee Evans for his suggestions and to Paul Sheftel for his assistance with the recording.*

# SUNDAY IN LONDON TOWN

Secondo

music by George Gershwin
words by Clifford Grey
arranged by Jim Lyke

# SUNDAY IN LONDON TOWN

## Primo

music by George Gershwin
words by Clifford Grey
arranged by Jim Lyke

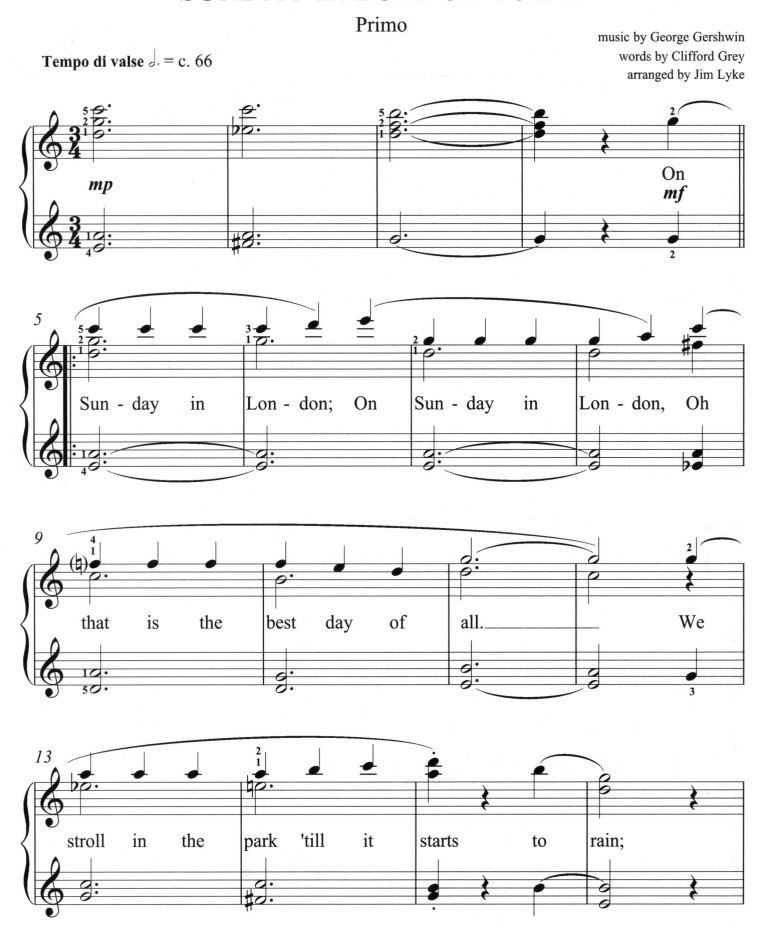

wait 'till it stops then we go out a - gain

It's

hi - did - dle did - dle, Our thumbs we can twid - dle

2423

# YANKEE DOODLE BLUES

### Secondo

Music by George Gershwin
Words by B. G. DeSylva
Arranged by Jim Lyke

# YANKEE DOODLE BLUES

## Primo

Music by George Gershwin
Words by B. G. DeSylva
Arranged by Jim Lyke

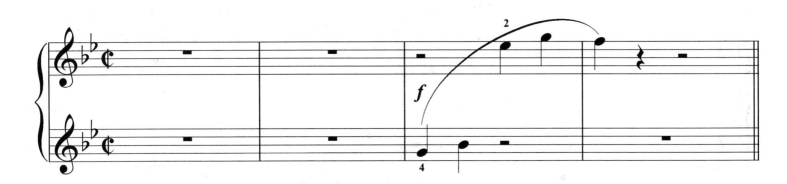

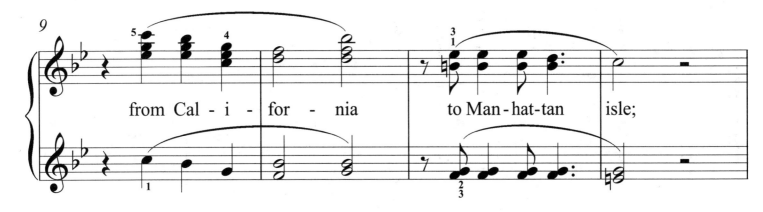

Secondo

*When I hear*

*Yan-kee Doo-dle* *that mel-o - dy* *keeps on ring-ing in my ear;*

*"Yan-kee Doo- dle,"* *that mel-o-dy* *makes me stand right up and cheer,*

# THEY DIDN'T BELIEVE ME

## Secondo

Music by Jerome Kern
Words by Herbert Reynolds
Arranged by Jim Lyke

# THEY DIDN'T BELIEVE ME

## Primo

Music by Jerome Kern
Words by Herbert Reynolds
Arranged by Jim Lyke

lov - li - est girl that one could see!

That I'm the man whose wife one day you'll be They'll nev - er be-

lieve me, They'll nev - er be-lieve me That from this great big world you've

chos - en me!

me!

# I LOVE A PIANO

## Secondo

Words and Music by Irving Berlin
Arranged by Jim Lyke

Moderately Slow ( ♩ = 80 )

# I LOVE A PIANO

## Primo

Words and Music by Irving Berlin
Arranged by Jim Lyke

Secondo

2423

# LOOK FOR THE SILVER LINING

## Secondo

Music by Jerome Kern
Words by B.G. DeSylva
Arranged by Jim Lyke

Moderately ($\bf{o}$ = 60)

some where___ the sun is shin - ing___ And so the

# LOOK FOR THE SILVER LINING

## Primo

Music by Jerome Kern
Words by B.G. DeSylva
Arranged by Jim Lyke

2423

right thing    to  do    is make    it   shine   for you.    A

2423

# WHEN THE CURTAIN FALLS

(Act One, Act Two, Act Three)

## Secondo

words and music by Irving Berlin
arranged by Jim Lyke

**Moderato** ♩ = 120

# WHEN THE CURTAIN FALLS

(Act One, Act Two, Act Three)

## Primo

words and music by Irving Berlin
arranged by Jim Lyke

part - ed,_____ for one long year._____

spend - ing,_____ a hap - py end - ing_____

We see them

# I'LL BUILD A STAIRWAY TO PARADISE

Secondo

Music by George Gershwin
Words by B. G. DeSylva and Ira Gershwin
Arranged by Jim Lyke

# I'LL BUILD A STAIRWAY TO PARADISE

## Primo

Music by George Gershwin
Words by B. G. DeSylva and Ira Gershwin
Arranged by Jim Lyke

Moderato ( ♩ = c. 110 )

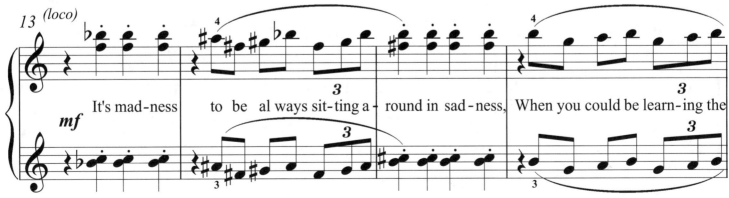

2423

Secondo

Primo

Secondo

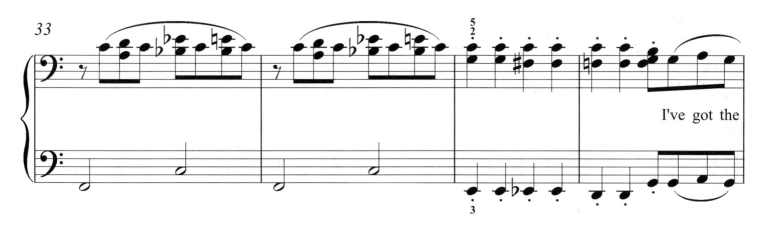

I've got the

blues

## Composer Biographies

The three composers represented in this collection of show tunes and movie tunes for piano duet wrote in an era that became known as the Golden Age of American Popular Song. This period began roughly in the mid 1920's and lasted until the advent of rock music in the 1960's. Gershwin, Kern, and Berlin wrote songs for Broadway musicals as well as Hollywood musicals. Their songs became "standards" (usually in a 32 bar format) and favorites of jazz musicians who improvised on the harmonic scheme of the songs. Famous singers (Frank Sinatra, Ella Fitzgerald, Harry Connick, Jr. etc.) keep the songs from this era alive today. When performing the songs in this album, study the lyrics. The lyrics will help you shape phrases and build an effective interpretation.

**George Gershwin** (1898-1937). Gershwin grew up in New York's lower East Side and received excellent training in piano and harmony. He was attracted to the music of Kern and Berlin and started writing for Broadway musicals at a very young age. His first "hit" song, **Swanee**, sold a million copies in sheet music. His brother, Ira, became Gershwin's preferred lyricist. Together, they wrote many hit shows for Broadway, and later, Hollywood musicals. Gershwin also wrote serious music including **Rhapsody in Blue**, **Piano Concerto in F**, and **An American In Paris**. His musical, **Porgy and Bess**, is considered a masterpiece and has become a staple in opera houses in America and Europe. Gershwin died at a very young age while composing music for Hollywood films.

**Jerome Kern** (1885-1945). Kern was born in New York to an affluent family. He studied at the New York College of Music and also in Germany. He and Gershwin shared the same experience as rehearsal pianists for Broadway musicals. His song, **Look for the Silver Lining** (in this album) is from the musical, **Sally**. Like Gershwin, Kern composed music for many Hollywood musicals. He worked with the noted lyricist Oscar Hammerstein, II. In 1927, they wrote the musical **Showboat**. This musical was a landmark in Broadway musicals in that it integrated the plot with the music in a fresh way and touched upon controversial issues. Kern won two Academy Awards in Hollywood for the songs **The Way You Look Tonight** and **The Last Time I Saw Paris**. Perhaps his best known song is **All the Things You Are**.

**Irving Berlin** (1888-1989). Berlin grew up in the lower East Side of New York in abject poverty. He began his career in music as a singing waiter and taught himself to play the piano. His first "hit" song was **Alexander's Ragtime Band** which sold over a million copies. He founded his own publishing company and later built, with his business partner, Sam Harris, the Music Box Theatre on Broadway as a showcase for his musical reviews. Like Kern and Gershwin, he was involved with Hollywood musicals and composed scores for Fred Astaire musicals. His most famous Broadway musical, **Annie Get Your Gun**, produced the show business anthem, **There's No Business Like Show Business**. Other Berlin songs include **God Bless America** and **Blue Skies**. Berlin lived to be 101 years old.